A   B

H

N

Charlip, Remy
Handtalk.

T

Y   Z

YOU DON'T HAVE TO USE YOUR VOICE TO TALK. YOU CAN TALK WITH YOUR EYES, YOUR FACE, YOUR HANDS, YOUR BODY.

THE AMERICAN INDIANS USED TO TALK THIS WAY WHEN THEY DIDN'T KNOW THE LANGUAGE OF ANOTHER TRIBE.

THIS IS THE FIRST BOOK OF ITS KIND FOR YOUNG PEOPLE ON TWO WAYS THAT DEAF PEOPLE TALK: *FINGER SPELLING*, FORMING WORDS LETTER BY LETTER WITH THE FINGERS OF ONE HAND, AND *SIGNING*, MAKING A PICTURE OR SIGN WITH ONE OR TWO HANDS FOR EACH WORD OR IDEA.

YOU ALREADY KNOW MANY *HANDTALK* SIGNS IN THIS BOOK, LIKE *BIG*, *CRAZY*, *HELLO*.

A SIGN STANDS FOR THE CONCEPT BEHIND THE WORD AS WELL AS THE WORD ITSELF, SO THAT YOU CAN MAKE *BIG* ALSO MEAN *LARGE*, *HUGE*, *ENORMOUS*, *GIGANTIC*, BY CHANGING THE FEELING OF THE GESTURE. DON'T BE AFRAID TO USE YOUR EYES, FACE, BODY, AND YOUR LEGS TO SHOW EXACTLY WHAT YOU MEAN.

SIGNS CHANGE WITH THE TIMES, AS WELL AS FROM PLACE TO PLACE. THE OLD SIGN FOR *TELEPHONE* USED TO BE MADE WITH TWO HANDS, ONE AT THE EAR AND ONE AT THE MOUTH. SOME PEOPLE DO *VAMPIRE* BY PLACING THE TWO FINGERS OF THE LETTER *V* TO THE SIDE OF THE NECK. THE SIGN FOR *AMERICA* IS DONE DIFFERENTLY IN ENGLAND, FRANCE, THE SOVIET UNION, AND THE UNITED STATES.

THE *HANDTALK* WORDS IN THIS BOOK ARE SIMPLE AND FUN TO DO. TRY THEM WITH A FRIEND, AND MAKE UP SOME NEW SIGNS IF YOU WANT TO HAVE A SECRET CODE. NOW YOU CAN TALK FROM FAR AWAY WITHOUT SHOUTING, FROM BEHIND CLOSED WINDOWS, AND EVEN UNDER WATER.

THIS IS ONLY A BEGINNING. THERE ARE OVER 5,000 SIGNS IN THE LANGUAGE OF THE DEAF. IT IS A RICH AND BEAUTIFUL LANGUAGE USED BY HUNDREDS OF THOUSANDS IN THE UNITED STATES ALONE.

IF YOU WANT TO LEARN MORE *HANDTALK* ASK A DEAF PERSON WHO KNOWS SIGN LANGUAGE TO SHOW YOU.

THIS WORK WAS MADE POSSIBLE THROUGH THE GENEROUS COOPERATION OF THE NATIONAL THEATRE OF THE DEAF AND THE EUGENE O'NEILL MEMORIAL THEATER CENTER, INC. THE NATIONAL THEATRE OF THE DEAF IS FUNDED, PRIMARILY, BY THE U.S. OFFICE OF EDUCATION, DEPARTMENT OF HEALTH, EDUCATION AND WELFARE. ALSO, THANKS TO TIMOTHY SCANLON, FREDA NORMAN, JOSEPH SARPY, DOROTHY MILES, FANNY YEH, ARTHUR TOMLINSON, MAX BURGESS, GUY WONDER AND ESPECIALLY NIKKI KILPATRICK AND DAVID HAYS DIRECTOR OF NTD.

HANDTALK

AN ABC OF FINGER SPELLING & SIGN LANGUAGE

REMY CHARLIP   MARY BETH   GEORGE ANCONA

PUBLISHED BY PARENTS' MAGAZINE PRESS NEW YORK, NEW YORK

TEXT COPYRIGHT © 1974 BY REMY CHARLIP AND MARY BETH MILLER
ILLUSTRATION COPYRIGHT © 1974 BY REMY CHARLIP
PHOTOGRAPHS COPYRIGHT © 1974 BY GEORGE ANCONA
ALL RIGHTS RESERVED. PRINTED IN THE UNITED STATES OF AMERICA
LIBRARY OF CONGRESS CATALOGING IN PUBLICATION DATA
CHARLIP, REMY.
HANDTALK: AN ABC OF FINGER SPELLING & SIGN LANGUAGE.
SUMMARY: AN INTRODUCTION TO TWO KINDS OF SIGN
LANGUAGE: FINGER SPELLING, OR FORMING WORDS LETTER
BY LETTER WITH THE FINGERS, AND SIGNING, OR MAKING
SIGNS WITH ONE OR TWO HANDS FOR EACH WORD OR IDEA.
1. SIGN LANGUAGE—JUVENILE LITERATURE.
[1. SIGN LANGUAGE. 2. ALPHABET BOOKS] I. MILLER, MARY BETH,
JOINT AUTHOR. II. ANCONA, GEORGE, JOINT AUTHOR. III. TITLE.
P135.C45   419   73-10199
ISBN 0-8193-0705-X   ISBN 0-8193-0706-8 (LIB. BDG.)

FOR MY FATHER CHESTER, MY MOTHER NELLIE, MY SISTER BEVERLY

A

ANGEL

B U G

B

BUTTER

C

D

E

F

G

H

I

STAND

SLIP

FALL

J

TWO FINGERS STAND, THEN GO UP, AND LAND AGAIN

K

L

N

NO

NO

NO

O

THE LETTER N AND YOU GET THE WORD NO.   O.K.?

NO   O   K

PEANUT

BUTTER

WHEN YOU CLOSE THESE PAGES

THESE

P

AND

JELLY

HANDS

MAKE THE SIGN FOR SANDWICH

Q

R

S

CIRCLE WITH FINGER, THEN OPEN SAME HAND

T

U

V

IN......... A......... VERY.......... UGLY........... VILLAGE...............

NEAR............... A......... VERY......... UGLY........... VALLEY..............

UNDER........ A......... VERY......... UGLY........... VOLCANO...............

LIVED............ A............... VERY.............. UGLY.............. VAMPIRE...........

WITH.......... HIS.......... BEAUTIFUL............. VULTURE.

MY NAME IS VALENTINE

W

OPEN AND CLOSE THE FINGERS OF ONE HAND LIKE THE SHUTTER
OF A CAMERA. IT IS ALSO THE SIGN FOR A FLASH OF LIGHT.

X

I

L

Y

COMBINE 3 LETTERS FOR SHORTHAND: I LOVE YOU

Y